24 Nonfiction Passages for Test Practice

Grades 6–8

by Michael Priestley

SCHOLASTIC

PROFESSIONAL BOOKS

New York • Toronto • London • Auckland • Sydney
Mexico City • New Delhi • Hong Kong • Buenos Aires

Cover design by Solás
Interior design by Creative Pages, Inc.
Interior illustration by Greg Harris, page 40
Interior photos by Schweiger/Arendt/OKAPIA/Photo Researchers, page 7; Elsa/Allsport, page 8; UPI/Bettman/Corbis, page 24; Reuters NewMedia Inc./Corbis, page 30; Culver Pictures, page 36

ISBN 0-439-25610-0

24 Nonfiction Passages for Test Practice
Grades 6–8

❦ Contents ❦

Introduction

Today's students receive information from an ever-increasing number of sources. To manage this overload of information, students must be able to distinguish between what is important and what is not—a key skill in reading nonfiction. They must understand what they read in traditional forms of nonfiction, such as textbooks and news articles, but they must also comprehend newer forms of nonfiction, such as advertisements on Web sites and e-mail on the Internet. Many students can benefit from reading more nonfiction, but finding good examples of nonfiction for instruction at different grade levels can be challenging.

How to Use This Book

The purpose of this book is to provide interesting, well-written nonfiction selections for students to read. These selections can be used for practice and instruction in reading nonfiction, and they can be used to help prepare students for taking tests that include nonfiction passages.

This book provides 24 grade-appropriate nonfiction texts in a wide variety of genres, from informational articles, letters, and biographies to e-mail announcements and how-to guides. Each text (of one to two pages) focuses on a high-interest topic and has:

- a prereading question to help students focus on what they read.
- a set of 2–6 comprehension questions that resemble the kinds of questions students will see on standardized tests.

The questions with these texts are designed to measure critical thinking and comprehension skills, such as summarizing information, drawing conclusions, and evaluating an author's purpose and point of view. These questions will help you assess students' comprehension of the material and will help students practice answering test questions. For different passages, questions include multiple-choice items, short-answer items, and written-response items that require longer answers. (You will find answers to these questions in the Answer Key beginning on page 46.)

Extending Activities

For some of these richly detailed texts, you may want to have students go beyond answering only the questions that are provided. For example, for any given text you could have students write a summary of the selection in their own words or rewrite the passage from a different point of view. For some pairs of texts, you might have students compare and contrast the two selections. For other texts, you might want to create writing prompts and have students write full-length essays about what they have learned. Students will benefit from reading and analyzing these texts, discussing them in class or in small groups, and writing about them in a variety of ways.

Name _____ Date _____

Text 1 Which taste better, mealworms or crickets?

Eating Bugs

Today's Menu
Mealworm bread
Ant brood tacos
Chocolate-covered
crickets

Some insects, such as butterflies and ladybugs, are quite beautiful. But, did you know that many bugs are also edible and are filled with protein?

Aletheia Price knows this—and a lot more—about bugs. She also thinks you should try eating some. If you visit the Web site www.eatbug.com, you will find all kinds of information about edible insects. Most of it was written by Aletheia Price when she was fifteen years old. Aletheia started eating bugs at the age of thirteen. Before long, she found that she really enjoyed some of them. She also became interested in finding out more about which kinds of bugs could be eaten and how to cook them.

According to Aletheia, there are at least 1,462 kinds of edible insects. (Doesn't that make you wonder who tried all of them and decided they were edible?) Some of her favorite dishes include mealworm chocolate chip cookies, ant tacos, and chocolate-covered crickets. On her Web site she offers information for anyone who wants to raise bugs for food. She also has recipes for insect entrees and some helpful tips. For example, Aletheia prefers eating cooked insects to live ones because she likes food that cannot crawl off her plate. Also, when preparing crickets, it is best to remove their legs before cooking. (The legs tend to get stuck in your teeth.)

Aletheia realizes that eating bugs is not for everyone. But, if you think about it, you have to admit that eating bugs might be a good idea. There are billions and billions of bugs in this world. If we could get used to eating them, we would have plenty of food for everyone.

1. **Which information can you find on the Web site www.eatbug.com?**
   Ⓐ the names of restaurants that serve bugs
   Ⓑ recipes for preparing food made with insects
   Ⓒ a list of 1,462 kinds of edible bugs
   Ⓓ suggestions for solving the world's hunger problems

2. **Based on what you have read here, how would you describe Aletheia Price? What kind of person is she? Tell why you think so.**

_____

_____

Text 2 Where can the skateboarders go?

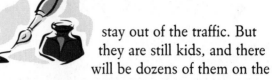

To the Editor:

As the owner of a local restaurant, I try to stay on good terms with the members of the community, both young and old. I encourage local people to spend time in downtown Burlington, and I also encourage young people to exercise as much as they can. However, having these same young people riding skateboards up and down our sidewalks, knocking over pedestrians, and generally being a real nuisance, is not exactly what I had in mind.

Right now, young people are skating on the sidewalks and in the parking lots after school and on weekends, but school will soon be out. What will happen then? I think we all know the answer. Kids will be riding up and down the streets all day long and into the evening.

Most of the skateboarding kids are polite and considerate. They try not to bother people walking on the sidewalks, and they stay out of the traffic. But they are still kids, and there will be dozens of them on the street as soon as school lets out. There are always a few troublemakers, too, and they will cause some problems.

I would like to suggest that we avoid the whole situation by doing something about it now. I think the best approach would be to build a skate park in the downtown area where kids can skate as much as they want. Such a park would provide a place for the kids to go and would help prevent accidents on the sidewalk and in the streets. I also think this can be done inexpensively. A skate park does not require a lot of resources, and I think many parents would contribute time and money to the project.

Martin LaPierre
Burlington

---

1. **What is the writer of this letter most concerned about?**
    (A) Young people do not have good manners.
    (B) There will soon be too many skateboarders on the sidewalks.
    (C) Students do not spend enough time in school.
    (D) Young people need more exercise.

2. **The writer's main purpose in this letter is to —**
    (F) help solve a problem.
    (G) praise the city.
    (H) compare young people of the past and present.
    (J) criticize the local government.

3. **List three positive reasons to support the idea of building a skate park.**

    _____

    _____

    _____

Text 3 What is a bearded dragon?

Subject: Bearded Dragons
Date: 9/1/00 12:24:32 PM EDT
From: LCW@scc.pet

Are you looking for the perfect pet? Have you ever met a bearded dragon?

Bearded dragons are reptiles that live in the desert. They are native to Australia, and they enjoy hot, dry weather. "Beardies" have become very popular pets because they are good-natured and easy to tame. They are also easy to care for. They need strong sunlight and warm temperatures. They eat insects, worms, fruits, and vegetables. For some part of each day, bearded dragons must be able to bask in the light with a temperature of about 100 degrees. This warmth not only keeps the animal happy, but basking is also necessary for good digestion.

An adult bearded dragon is 1–2 feet long and will generally live to an age of about eight years. Today you can buy BDs in many different colors, so you will want to choose your pet carefully. Popular kinds include Sandfire, German Giant, Golddust, Orange Tiger, Red Phase, and Red-Gold.

Bearded dragons are very social animals, and their behaviors can be quite interesting. A male BD, for example, will show its puffed-up beard to attract a female or to scare off other animals. BDs will often bob their heads and wave their arms, too, when they want to communicate.

If you are interested in buying a bearded dragon, visit our Web site. Or send us an e-mail, and we will send you a color catalog about bearded dragons. You will love having a BD as your pet!

1. **The main purpose of this e-mail is to —**
  Ⓐ tell an entertaining story about dragons.
  Ⓑ give information about animals of Australia.
  Ⓒ persuade you to buy a bearded dragon.
  Ⓓ compare bearded dragons with other animals.

2. **Bearded dragons sometimes communicate by —**
  Ⓕ waving their arms.   Ⓗ making loud noises.
  Ⓖ kicking their feet.   Ⓙ charging at people.

3. **Would a bearded dragon be a good pet for you? Explain why or why not.**

  _____

  _____

  _____

CAPTAIN CAMMI

When Team USA skated onto the ice at the 1998 Olympic Games in Nagano, Japan, few people expected the women's hockey squad to win the Gold Medal. Canada, their opponent in the final game, had beaten the U.S. team in every world championship tournament since 1990. But the Nagano tournament was different, and Team USA did win. The captain of the team and the one player most responsible for the victory was Catherine "Cammi" Granato.

Born in 1971, Cammi Granato grew up in Downers Grove, Illinois. From the age of five, there was nothing she enjoyed more than playing ice hockey with her four older brothers. In the school she attended, there were no girls' hockey teams, but that did not stop Cammi. She became good enough to play on the boys' teams instead.

In 1988, Cammi had an unusual opportunity. She got to watch her older brother Tony play for the U.S. men's hockey team in the Olympics. After that experience, Cammi was determined that one day, she would play in the Olympics herself, even though women's hockey was not an Olympic sport at that time.

After high school, Cammi Granato went to Providence College, and that's where she became a star. In her career at Providence, she became the school's all-time leading goal scorer with 139 goals and 117 assists. She helped lead her team to two national championships and was chosen ECAC Player of the Year for three straight years.

In 1990, Cammi Granato became a member of the first U.S. national women's hockey team, and she has been a member of every national team since then. She also became the national team's leading scorer with 30 goals and 22 assists in 25 games.

Cammi Granato has won many awards and has excelled in many important hockey games, but for her, none was more important or more meaningful than the final game at Nagano in 1998. Her personal dream had come true. She not only got to play in the Olympics, but she and her team won the Gold Medal. According to Cammi, winning that gold medal was the greatest thing she had ever achieved.

Since Nagano, Cammi Granato has been playing with the U.S. national team. She has also appeared in television commercials and has attended many events to help promote women's hockey. In 1999, she also became a radio commentator for the Los Angeles Kings of the National Hockey League. That must have been great fun at times—especially when the Kings played against her brother Tony, a member of the San Jose Sharks.

Scholastic Professional Books

1. **Team USA was not expected to win the Gold Medal at the 1998 Olympics because —**

   (A) the U.S. team had lost to Canada several times before.

   (B) Cammi Granato was the captain of the team.

   (C) the game was played in Nagano, Japan.

   (D) Cammi Granato was at Providence College at the time.

2. **In grade school, Cammi Granato played on boys' hockey teams because —**

   (F) the girls' teams were not very good.

   (G) she wanted to play against her brothers.

   (H) the boys' teams could not win without her.

   (J) there were no girls' hockey teams at that time.

3. **On the lines below, write three of Cammi Granato's most important achievements.**

   1. _____

   2. _____

   3. _____

4. **How did Cammi's brothers influence her own hockey career?**

   _____

   _____

   _____

   _____

Feng Shui

At the Whitney Museum of American Art in New York City, the most popular items for sale in the gift shop this year were stone lions. These lions were made by Chinese artist Cai Guo-Qiang. But people could not just buy them. Customers had to explain why they needed the lions. Cai chose the customers he thought needed the lions most. Then, for a cost of $500 to $1,000 each, Cai sold the stone lions with directions on where to place them.

The popularity of the stone lions is related to *feng shui* (pronounced "fung shway"), which is an old Chinese tradition. The words mean "wind and water." The practice of feng shui involves types of energy and where they are located. Believers feel that you will be successful in life if you arrange your home and place of business in the best possible ways. A good arrangement will attract good energy, and your life will be good. If your home is arranged poorly, bad energy will follow.

Ten years ago, not many people in this country believed in feng shui. But that has changed. Especially in large cities, such as New York and Los Angeles, more and more people now hire feng shui experts to help them find the right homes and improve their lives. But how does feng shui work?

The picture at the right shows where to find the eight important "life stations." Now imagine that your home is a square, and the front door is the "Career" station. The other shape stations are located in

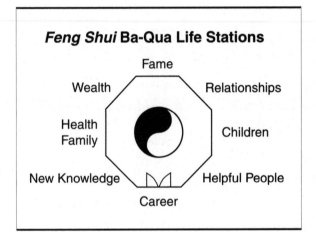

Feng Shui Ba-Qua Life Stations

relation to the front door. What you place in each location will determine how successful you are. For example, the far left corner is the location for "Wealth." If you have healthy plants growing in that part of your house, then your wealth will grow. If you have a pile of dirty laundry in that corner, then you will have little success in business.

The same kinds of principles apply in other life stations. Plants, crystals, lights, mirrors, and candles are things that attract good energy. Half-moon shapes, the sun, bells, and chimes are good, too. Stones (like the stone lions), trees, and lamp stands add strength to your home. But long halls, fans, toilets, TVs, and such can block energy. They must be placed carefully or removed. Also, piles of junk must be cleaned up and toys put away. Everything should be in order.

Does the practice of feng shui really work? No one can say for sure. But paying attention to where you put things and cleaning up piles of junk will probably improve your life anyway. So why not try it?

Scholastic Professional Books

1. The traditions of feng shui first came from —
   Ⓐ New York City.
   Ⓑ China.
   Ⓒ Los Angeles.
   Ⓓ France.

2. According to the article, which of these would attract "good" energy?
   Ⓕ an electric fan
   Ⓖ a television
   Ⓗ wind chimes
   Ⓙ piles of toys

3. Explain the main principles of feng shui in your own words.

   _____

   _____

   _____

   _____

4. If you wanted to find more information about feng shui, which of these would be the best place to look?
   Ⓐ dictionary
   Ⓑ *Readers' Guide to Periodical Literature*
   Ⓒ thesaurus
   Ⓓ social studies textbook

5. Do you think that feng shui might help you in your life? Give a reason for your opinion.

   _____

   _____

   _____

TEXT 6 *What is gazpacho?*

MAKING GAZPACHO

R eal Mexican cuisine is colorful and spicy. It combines the best foods of Spain and the Native American cuisine of the Aztecs. Try this fine recipe for gazpacho, a tomato-based soup that is served cold.

Gazpacho

2 large tomatoes, peeled	3 cups tomato juice	1/8 teaspoon black pepper
1 large cucumber, pared	1/3 cup olive oil	2 cloves garlic
1 medium onion	1/3 cup red-wine vinegar	1/2 cup croutons
1 medium green pepper	1/4 teaspoon Tabasco	1/4 cup chopped chives
1 pimiento, drained	1 1/2 teaspoons salt	

1. Combine one tomato, one-half each of the cucumber, onion, and green pepper, one pimiento, and 1/2 cup tomato juice in a blender. With the cover on, blend this mixture at high speed for 30 seconds.
2. Next, put the mixture in a large bowl. Add 1/4 cup olive oil, vinegar, Tabasco, salt and pepper, and the remaining tomato juice. With the bowl covered, refrigerate for 2 hours until well chilled.
3. While the vegetables chill, rub the inside of a frying pan with garlic (save the garlic). Add the rest of the olive oil to the pan and heat. Then sauté the croutons until they are browned.
4. Chop the remaining tomato, cucumber, onion, and pepper. Place them in separate bowls. Along with bowls for the croutons and chopped chives, serve as accompaniments.
5. When you are ready to serve the chilled soup, crush the garlic you saved and add it to the soup. Mix the soup well and serve in bowls.

Makes 6 servings.

1. The author of this recipe states that Mexican food is "colorful and spicy." Do you think that gazpacho fits this description? Tell why.

_____

_____

2. Why does the recipe tell you in step 3 to "save the garlic"?

_____

_____

Scholastic Professional Books

Text 7 Will the Leaning Tower of Pisa fall over?

The Leaning Tower

VOLUME X   Anyplace, USA   **Monday, June 18**

PISA, Italy—Engineers said last week that they have stopped the sinking of the famous Leaning Tower of Pisa. The tower has been closed since 1990 for fear that it would someday fall over. Now, according to project leader Paolo Heiniger, the tower has been fixed. But it still leans.

This city in Italy would not be the same if the Tower did not lean. Millions of tourists visit Pisa every year to see the 196-foot tower. Until ten years ago, people could also climb to the top of the tower. Some people believe that is where Galileo did his experiments with gravity nearly 500 years ago.

Construction of the tower began in 1173 when Pisa was a center of power and wealth. But work was stopped several times because of wars. The eight-story tower was not completed until the late 1200s. Even then, the tower leaned.

The tower itself is made of marble and weighs 16,000 tons. Problems in the construction of the tower were caused by the soil underneath. The ground is softer on one side than on the other. The entire tower has been slowly sinking into the ground for centuries. The south side has sunk 6.1 feet below ground level. The north side has sunk 12.3 feet!

Now, engineers have completed the 20 million dollar project. They have removed soil from under one side of the tower and pulled the tower a bit more upright. These corrections should keep the tower standing for another 300 years.

1. **What is the main idea of this article?**
    Ⓐ Paolo Heiniger is the project leader working on the Tower of Pisa.
    Ⓑ The city of Pisa was once a center of power and wealth.
    Ⓒ Construction of the Tower of Pisa took more than one hundred years.
    Ⓓ The Tower of Pisa was in danger of falling over, but engineers have fixed the problem.

2. **Which detail supports the idea that the Leaning Tower is important to the economy of Pisa?**
    Ⓕ Millions of people visit Pisa every year to see the tower.
    Ⓖ The eight-story tower was not completed until the late 1200s.
    Ⓗ Now the tower will stand for another 300 years.
    Ⓙ Engineers have removed soil from under one side of the tower.

3. **Why does the tower of Pisa lean?**

    _____

Scholastic Professional Books

Text 8 Should you see this movie?

Chicken Run

When a hen named Ginger decides that she wants to flee the farm, she will not give up. However, she will not even think about escaping by herself. As far as she is concerned, all the chickens on the farm must escape at the same time. Ginger tries digging under the fence. She tries catapulting over it. She tries breaking through it. But each plan fails to get her and her clucking companions out of their "prison."

Just when Ginger is beginning to lose hope, along comes Rocky. He is an American rooster who likes to call himself the "lone free ranger." He promises to teach Ginger and her poultry pals to fly so they can escape. The fun really begins when Rocky tries to live up to his promise.

When the farmer's wife, Mrs. Tweedy, decides that she will stop selling eggs and begin making chicken pies, Ginger and her fowl friends face a desperate situation.

If you have not seen *Chicken Run* yet, see it soon. This is a remarkable movie made by Aardman Animations, led by Peter Lord and his partner, Nick Park. The Aardman crew made this movie by using a very slow process called "stop motion animation." All the characters in the movie are made of clay and other materials. Each scene is set up and filmed one at a time. Each camera shot makes up 1/24th of a second of film. Then the animators make tiny changes in the scene and take the next shot. A good solid week of hard work might yield one or two minutes of actual film for the movie. The entire movie took 18 months to complete.

Knowing what was involved in shooting this film makes it all the more amazing. With goofy characters that the kids will love and some very witty jokes for adults, this movie has something for everyone.

1. **In the movie, Ginger's main goal is to —**
    (A) find Rocky.
    (B) leave the chicken farm.
    (C) visit America.
    (D) learn how to fly.

2. **This movie took a long time to make because it was —**
    (F) filmed in color.
    (G) a complicated story.
    (H) animated.
    (J) made in England.

3. **Do you think you would enjoy watching the movie *Chicken Run*? Tell why or why not.**

    _____

    _____

Text 9 *What did Lincoln say in his speech?*

Speech to the One Hundred Sixty-Sixth Ohio Regiment

In 1864, Abraham Lincoln was president of the United States, and our country was caught up in the Civil War. On August 22 of that year, President Lincoln made this speech to some soldiers from Ohio who were returning home from the war.

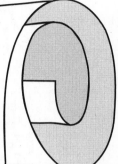

I suppose you are going home to see your families and friends. For the service you have done in this great struggle in which we are engaged I present you sincere thanks for myself and the country. I almost always feel inclined, when I happen to say anything to soldiers, to impress upon them in a few brief remarks the importance of success in this contest. It is not merely for to-day, but for all times to come that we should perpetuate for our children's children this great and free government, which we have enjoyed all our lives. I beg you to remember this, not merely for my sake, but for yours. I happen temporarily to occupy this big White House. I am a living witness that any one of your children may look to come here as my father's child has. It is in order that each of you may have through this free government which we have enjoyed, an open field and a fair chance for your industry, enterprise and intelligence; that you may all have equal privileges in the race of life, with all its desirable human aspirations. It is for this the struggle should be maintained, that we may not lose our birthright—not only for one, but for two or three years. The nation is worth fighting for, to secure such an inestimable jewel.

1. **What was the main purpose of this speech?**

    _____

    _____

2. **What did Lincoln say about the soldiers' children, compared with himself?**

    _____

    _____

3. **According to Lincoln, what was the most important reason to continue the struggle in the Civil War?**

    _____

    _____

Vermont Foliage Video

Only $19.95

Every year, thousands of people from all over the world travel to Vermont and other parts of New England to see the colorful autumn leaves. Now you can have the same experience in the comfort of your own home. When you buy this video, you will see the most beautiful autumn foliage in the world. And you can see this breathtaking scenery over and over again—whenever you want to!

Autumn in Vermont will take you to the loveliest places in the state, including:

- Mount Mansfield, Vermont's highest peak
- Green Mountain State Forest
- Camel's Hump, an unusual mountain peak reaching 4,083 feet
- The lakes of the Northeast Kingdom
- Lake Champlain, one of the largest lakes in the country

You will also visit Bennington, the site of an important battle during the American Revolution, and Plymouth, the birthplace of President Calvin Coolidge.

You will never forget the beauty of Vermont's foliage. Order now!

To mail in your order, send your name and address with a check for $19.95 plus $5.00 shipping and handling to: Autumn in Vermont, P.O. Box 7073, Leaftown, VT 00345.

100% satisfaction guaranteed. If you are not completely satisfied with your video, we will refund the purchase price—no questions asked.

Scholastic Professional Books

1. The main purpose of this text is to —
- Ⓐ give information about Vermont.
- Ⓑ persuade you to buy the video.
- Ⓒ compare Vermont with other states.
- Ⓓ explain how to get to Vermont.

2. Where would you be most likely to see this text?
- Ⓕ in a magazine
- Ⓖ on television
- Ⓗ in a textbook
- Ⓙ on the Internet

3. If you want to order the video *Autumn in Vermont,* what should you do? Describe how you would order.

_____

_____

_____

4. Describe three or four things you would see if you watched the video *Autumn in Vermont.*

_____

_____

_____

_____

5. What will the video company do if you don't like *Autumn in Vermont?*

_____

_____

Text 11 Why did people go mad over tulips?

Tulipomania

When most Americans think of the Netherlands, a country that is also called *Holland*, they think of tulips. In fact, Holland produces about three billion tulip bulbs each year, and Americans buy about one billion of those bulbs. But tulips did not originally grow in Holland. How they got there and became so popular is a tale so strange it is hard to believe.

The brilliantly colored flowers now known as Dutch tulips first came to Europe in the 1500s. They came mainly from Turkey and parts of Central Asia. In Turkey, tulips had been cultivated for centuries. In fact, the name *tulip* comes from the Turkish word *tülbent*, referring to a kind of hat worn by many Turks and Persians of that time. The hat and the flower were similar in shape.

The first tulip bulbs were brought to Holland in 1593 by a botanist named Carolus Clusius. He planted the bulbs and grew beautiful flowers. But he would not share his bulbs with anyone. Several "businessmen" who saw the flowers also saw an opportunity to make money. They visited Clusius's garden in the middle of the night and stole most of his bulbs. That was the beginning of a remarkable mania for tulip bulbs that created some huge fortunes in Holland—and then destroyed them.

By 1624, several kinds of tulips were being grown in Holland, but only in small numbers. The gorgeous flowers were very popular, especially those with unusual colors or stripes. Very rare kinds of tulips were even given important-sounding names, such as "Semper Augustus." Since there were so few bulbs available, however, they were very expensive. Only the wealthiest citizens could afford to buy them. Such demand made the tulip bulb a status symbol—people simply *had* to have them—and prices began to rise. When merchants and tradesmen saw how much money rich people would spend on tulip bulbs, they began planting and raising bulbs in any soil they could find. From this point on, the tulip business became a madness.

One of the most expensive kinds of tulip in 1624 was the "Semper Augustus." Its flowers had maroon and white stripes. This kind of tulip sold for as much as 3,000 guilders per bulb, or about 1,500 U.S. dollars. In 1624, that was a huge amount of money! For 3,000 guilders, one could buy a fine house in the city of Amsterdam, or enough food to last a family for most of a year. Instead, the money was spent on tulip bulbs.

In a very short time, hundreds of Dutch merchants became very wealthy men. Buying and selling tulips had become a national <u>mania</u>. People sold tulip bulbs that were still in the ground and had never bloomed, and the prices for them continued to go up and up for years. By 1634, merchants were selling rare types of tulip bulbs by weight. The larger, more mature bulbs cost a small fortune. Tulip merchants could make as much as $10,000 per week, often by buying and selling bulbs that no one had ever actually seen!

In 1637, the tulip trade reached its peak, and then it quickly tumbled. One day a group of tulip merchants suddenly could not find customers willing to pay the usual high prices for bulbs. Word spread quickly, and the bottom fell out of the market. People who were wealthy the day before were now bankrupt. The tulip craze came to an end.

1. **Which of these events happened first?**

Ⓐ A "Semper Augustus" bulb was sold for 3,000 guilders.

Ⓑ Several Dutch businessmen stole some tulip bulbs.

Ⓒ Clusius brought some tulip bulbs to Holland.

Ⓓ Merchants began selling tulip bulbs by weight.

2. **The article says, "Buying and selling tulips had become a national <u>mania</u>." The word <u>mania</u> means —**

Ⓕ a disease that infects tulips.

Ⓖ an unreasonable fondness or madness; craze.

Ⓗ a state of great happiness; joy.

Ⓙ an unusual kind of flower.

3. **Write a brief summary of how the tulip craze in Holland began and how it ended.**

_____

_____

_____

_____

Text 12 What happened to the city of Galveston in 1900?

LEARNING FROM HISTORY

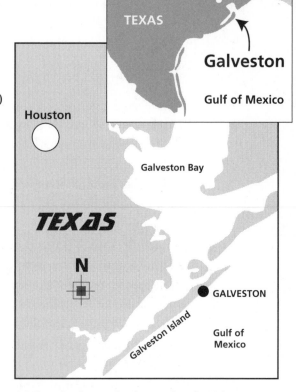

September 6, 1900. A terrible storm struck the Gulf of Mexico and was headed toward the coast of Texas. A hurricane watch was posted for the southern coast of the United States.

September 7, 1900. Heavy rain began to fall at 4:00 A.M. By 9:00 A.M., winds had increased, and huge waves began pounding the shores of Galveston Island. The Weather Bureau posted hurricane warnings, and nearly 20,000 people evacuated the island. Unfortunately, thousands of others paid no attention to the warning. Many people from Houston rode the train to Galveston to see the hurricane and watch the enormous waves. When the waves destroyed the boardwalk and smashed several wooden boats to pieces, people on the island realized it was time to leave. For most of them, it was already too late.

September 8, 1900. By 3:00 A.M., winds had reached 125 miles per hour. The three bridges connecting Galveston Island with the mainland had all been destroyed, so there was no way to escape. Waves more than 20 feet high crushed wooden buildings, houses, and ships. People fled to the center of the island, which was slightly higher than the shore, but it was no use. By early morning, most of the island was 15 feet under water. The only remaining structure above water was the Bolivar Point lighthouse, and it was overflowing with more people than it could hold.

September 9, 1900. As the storm began to move away from Galveston, the extent of the disaster became clear. More than 8,000 people died on Galveston Island in a period of 24 hours, most of them by drowning. More than 2,600 houses and over 12 square blocks of the city were completely demolished. There was no trace of these structures left. All bridges to the island and 15 miles of railroad track were destroyed, and the few people who survived on the island had no way to communicate with people on the mainland. The only functioning structure left was the Bolivar Point lighthouse. Its beacon shined for several days to help ships back to shore and to tell people on the mainland that there were survivors on the island who needed help.

After this massive storm, the people of Galveston immediately began to rebuild the city. First they worked to raise the elevation of the island to a few feet above sea level. Then they constructed a concrete seawall that was 17 feet high and 3 miles long.

Galveston soon became a thriving city once again, and it is thriving today. For decades, most of the construction in Galveston has stayed behind the seawall. But now, as the population continues to grow and oceanfront homes become more popular, people are once again building houses on the beach. The lessons learned from the great hurricane of 1900 have faded into the past.

1. **On September 7, people from Houston took the train to Galveston because they wanted to —**
  (A) escape from the storm.
  (B) see the hurricane.
  (C) help the people of Galveston rebuild.
  (D) visit the lighthouse.

2. **By September 8, thousands of people could not leave Galveston because —**
  (F) the trains were running behind schedule.
  (G) they refused to leave their homes behind.
  (H) the lighthouse was no longer working.
  (J) bridges to the mainland had been washed out.

3. **Which statement from the passage is an opinion?**
  (A) "Heavy rain began to fall at 4:00 A.M."
  (B) "People fled to the center of the island, which was slightly higher."
  (C) "Galveston soon became a thriving city once again."
  (D) "They constructed a seawall that was 17 feet high and 3 miles long."

4. **What lesson do you think people learned from the hurricane of 1900?**

_____

_____

_____

5. **What does the author of this passage think of the people who are now building oceanfront homes in Galveston? Explain.**

_____

_____

_____

Text 13 What did Harry Truman write in his letters?

President Harry Truman loved to write letters. Between 1910 and 1959, he wrote more than 1,200 letters to Elizabeth Wallace, whom he married in 1919. Below is an excerpt from a letter he wrote to "Bessie" long before he became President.

Grandview, Mo.
February 13, 1912

Dear Bessie:

Since this is your birthday and tomorrow is St. Valentine's and I have neither a present nor a valentine good enough to send you, I shall try and make some amends by sending you a very ordinary letter. Which all sounds very stilted and set just as if it was copied from some ancient work on how to write letters. Doesn't it? Well any*how* (with emphasis on the how) I wanted to send you something but hadn't brains enough to think of anything decent enough that would properly fit my present assets. So I thought I would get nothing and just tell you about it. That probably won't do you any good but then a good intention ought to count for something. . . .

I heard a man tell another one on the train last night, that he would have stolen a Bible if he could have gotten it to go into his pocket. Then he went on to describe what a fine one it was with a red leather back and fine wood engravings. Said he wanted it most awful bad but the owner watched him so closely he couldn't get away with it. Now, I think a man ought to draw the line at stealing a Bible. Of course I suppose it is no worse to steal one than it is to steal any other book or piece of furniture, but it sounds rather sacrilegious, to say the least. I am sure if I were in the stealing business, I'd be rather superstitious about stealing one. . . .

The heavenly geese are certainly shedding feathers around this neighborhood this morning. About two inches of them have fallen already. I guess old man winter is going to stay until March, sure enough. We sure ought to produce a crop out of all proportion to former ones if hard winters count for much! All the oldest inhabitants say they do. . . .

Anyway, I hope you'll live a thousand years if you want to and never get a day older than you are.

I shall call you up Friday as soon as I can get to a phone and you can decide if I shall come for you or not. . . .

Please, I think you owe me a letter even if this concoction is a substitute for something else.

Sincerely,
Harry

1. **The tone of most of this letter is —**
   - (A) apologetic.
   - (B) angry.
   - (C) friendly.
   - (D) mournful.

2. **Harry Truman's main purpose in writing this letter to Bessie was to —**
   - (F) make up for not getting her anything for her birthday.
   - (G) tell her about the birthday present he bought for her.
   - (H) ask what kind of present she wanted for her birthday.
   - (J) remind her that the next day was St. Valentine's Day.

3. **What did Harry Truman get Bessie for her birthday?**

   _____

4. **What did Harry Truman think about someone stealing a Bible?**

   _____

   _____

   _____

5. **What does the third paragraph of this letter mean? In your own words, write one to two sentences telling what the paragraph means.**

   _____

   _____

   _____

6. **What did Harry Truman hope Bessie would do when she received this letter?**

   _____

   _____

The King of Soccer

Most people have never heard of the name Edson Arantes do Nascimento, but they have heard of Pelé. Without question, Pelé is the greatest soccer player ever. Edson Arantes do Nascimento and Pelé are two names for the same man.

Pelé was born on October 23, 1940, in Três Corações, a small village in Brazil. Soccer is the most popular sport in Brazil, and like most other children his age, Pelé grew up playing soccer. Too poor to afford a soccer ball, Pelé and his playmates often made one by tying together a bunch of rags. Their playing field was usually a sidewalk. Old tin cans marked where the goalposts should be.

Pelé and the other boys from his neighborhood often dreamed of one day becoming professional soccer players. They formed a neighborhood soccer team, calling it the September 7 team after the name of the street where they lived. At the age of eleven, Pelé was discovered by Waldemar de Brito, a former professional player. De Brito was then coach of the Bauru Soccer Club. He signed Pelé to play for the junior Bauru team.

In 1956, when Pelé was fifteen, de Brito took him to the city of Santos, Brazil, to try out for the Santos professional team. Pelé immediately distinguished himself as one of the better players, and he was not even sixteen years old yet. Coincidentally, Pelé's first game with Santos was on September 7—the name of the street he once lived on, the name of his first team, and the date of Brazil's National Independence Day.

In 1957, when Pelé was sixteen, he was selected to play on Brazil's national team. He scored the only goal for Brazil in the first game and another goal in the second game. Then in 1958, Pelé helped Brazil win its first World Cup.

Between 1958 and 1970, Pelé played in four World Cups. He is the only person to have played on three winning World Cup teams. Pelé played his last game with the Brazilian national team in 1971, but he continued to play for the Santos team for three more years before calling it quits.

Throughout his career, Pelé had an amazing ability to move people. Everybody wanted to see him play. In 1969, a war in Nigeria was stopped for two days because the Santos team had been invited to play there and people on both sides were so eager to see Pelé play.

Scholastic Professional Books

When Pelé retired in 1974, people thought he was leaving the game for good, but six months later he signed up to play for the New York Cosmos in the United States. He came to the United States, in part, to help promote the game of soccer, and he agreed to play for the Cosmos until the end of 1977.

Pelé was awarded the 1978 International Peace Award and was named Athlete of the Century in 1980. He also was inducted into the Black Athletes Hall of Fame in 1975 and into the United States Soccer Hall of Fame in 1993. Most recently, Pelé was named the National Olympics Committee's top athlete, even though he never competed in the Olympics!

Pelé's name has become synonymous with excellence in soccer. His 20-year career has yielded some of the most memorable moments in soccer history. People today still refer to him as the great Pelé, the King of Soccer.

1. **Which event happened first?**
  Ⓐ Pelé was selected to play on Brazil's national team.
  Ⓑ Pelé agreed to play for the New York Cosmos.
  Ⓒ Pelé tried out for the Santos professional team.
  Ⓓ Pelé was discovered by Waldemar de Brito.

2. **What did Pelé do that no other person has ever done?**

_____

_____

3. **In 1969, a war in Nigeria was stopped for two days because —**
  Ⓕ Pelé refused to play there unless the fighting stopped.
  Ⓖ people on both sides wanted to see Pelé play soccer.
  Ⓗ Nigerians did not want Pelé to be injured.
  Ⓙ people on both sides grew tired of fighting.

4. **Why did September 7 have a special meaning for Pelé? Give at least two reasons.**

_____

_____

Fireworks

We all love watching fireworks, from the flashy shows on the Fourth of July to the Roman candle burning in the backyard. But let's stop and think about the price we pay for just a few minutes of excitement.

First, the amount of money we spend on fireworks is absurd. The excitement is gone, literally, in a flash. Let's face it, what we really are doing is burning money. Yet, year after year, thousands of cities and towns spend our tax dollars for fireworks displays. Those tax dollars would be put to much better use feeding our hungry and housing our homeless.

Second, there is the matter of pollution. Fireworks contain chemicals that are harmful to people and animals. Over the years, these chemicals will poison the air we breathe and the water we drink.

Third, let's consider the trash left behind after a fireworks display. What a mess! One would expect that those who set off the fireworks would have the decency to pick up the trash afterwards. But they don't. The mess they leave behind reflects the kind of attitude many Americans have toward our environment.

Fourth, fireworks are dangerous. Some fireworks can damage your hearing, especially the fireworks used in public displays that give off a big BANG. Losing your hearing is too high a price to pay.

Despite all the safety warnings, we still see injuries and deaths as a result of fireworks. Approximately 10,000 Americans are injured every year by fireworks. According to the Council on Fireworks Safety, children from the ages of five to fourteen are the ones most often injured. Those sparklers that seem so harmless cause 10% of the injuries. But sparklers run a distant third after skyrockets (number two) and firecrackers, which are the leading cause of injuries.

In my view, all consumer fireworks should be banned. Public fireworks displays should be kept to a minimum and should be paid for through volunteer funding, not tax dollars. Finally, those people in charge of fireworks displays should be responsible for cleaning up the mess they make.

1. **What is the tone of this editorial?**

(A) sarcastic   (C) melancholy

(B) indifferent   (D) serious

2. **The author most likely wrote this editorial to —**

(F) express an opinion about fireworks.

(G) teach about fireworks safety.

(H) describe different types of fireworks.

(J) complain about noise during fireworks displays.

3. **According to the author, which type of fireworks are the leading cause of injuries?**

(A) Roman candles   (C) skyrockets

(B) sparklers   (D) firecrackers

4. **According to the author, how are fireworks harmful? Give one or two examples.**

_____

_____

_____

5. **Does the author of this editorial believe that all fireworks should be banned? Explain your answer.**

_____

_____

_____

6. **With which of the following statements would the author most likely agree?**

(F) Public fireworks displays should be paid for with tax dollars.

(G) The money we spend on fireworks would be better spent helping others.

(H) Hearing loss is a small price to pay for the excitement that fireworks provide.

(J) The small amounts of harmful chemicals found in fireworks are nothing to be concerned about.

Text 16 How does the U.S. Treasury keep people from making their own money?

Funny Money

Counterfeiting of paper money in the United States has quite a long history. Ever since people began using paper currency, criminals have been making fake money. During Colonial times, when each colony issued its own "notes" or bills, counterfeiting was a huge problem. Most of the Colonial bills were small and printed on only one side. The designs on them were fairly simple. Anyone with just a bit of skill and the right tools could copy them without too much trouble.

Counterfeiting was also a problem in the 1830s when up to 1,600 different banks were issuing paper money. There were so many different kinds of bills circulating that it was hard to pick out the counterfeits.

In the 1860s, the United States Treasury began issuing its own paper money. The government tried to design bills that would be hard to counterfeit. The bills were printed on cotton and linen paper with red and blue fibers running through it. The bills bore a Treasury seal and very elaborate designs. While these steps did help cut down on some of the counterfeiting, they did not put counterfeiters out of business.

Since 1877, the Department of the Treasury's Bureau of Engraving and Printing has printed all U.S. currency. But counterfeiting is still a problem. Today's thieves are quick to take advantage of new technology. For example, counterfeiters now use advanced copiers and printers to make copies of money, or they use a computer to scan images of the bills and print them out on desktop printers.

In 1990, the Bureau of Engraving and Printing introduced security threads and microprinting on its bills to try to prevent counterfeiting. In 1994, the government came up with better designs for bills. Newly designed $100 notes were issued in 1996, $50 notes in 1997, and $20 notes in 1998. The new $5 and $10 notes came out in 2000. The government does not plan to issue newly designed $1 bills since they are not popular with counterfeiters.

These new bills boast many features designed to help cut down on counterfeiting. One of them is a special ink that changes color when light hits the money at different angles. Another is microprinting of words that are so small, they are hard to duplicate.

Many people think the new bills look funny. The portraits on the front of the bills are much larger than before, and they are slightly off center. The new bills also have watermarks, which are based on the same art as the portrait. The watermarks can be seen from both sides when the bill is held up to a light, and they are extremely difficult to copy.

Preventing counterfeiting seems to be an ongoing battle. But who knows, it just might be this "funny money" that finally puts an end to the phony money business forever.

Scholastic Professional Books

1. **What is "counterfeiting"?**
    - Ⓐ printing real money
    - Ⓑ writing a bad check
    - Ⓒ making fake money
    - Ⓓ refusing to pay bills

2. **Why was it fairly easy to make counterfeit American money before 1860? Give at least two reasons.**

    _____

    _____

3. **Which of these events happened first?**
    - Ⓕ The Bureau of Engraving and Printing begin printing all U.S. currency.
    - Ⓖ The U.S. Treasury began issuing its own paper money.
    - Ⓗ Counterfeiters began making money with desktop printers.
    - Ⓙ The government put security threads into paper money.

4. **Why doesn't the government plan to issue any newly designed $1 bills?**
    - Ⓐ The bills are already too difficult for counterfeiters to copy.
    - Ⓑ The American people don't want any more "funny money."
    - Ⓒ The government plans to replace the bills with coins.
    - Ⓓ There is not enough profit in $1 bills to interest counterfeiters.

5. **Name two or three features of the new bills that are designed to cut down on counterfeiting.**

    _____

    _____

    _____

TRAVELING SUE

VOLUME XIII   Anyplace, USA   **Thursday, June 14**

Chicago, Illinois—The largest *Tyrannosaurus rex* fossil ever discovered is now a permanent exhibit at Chicago's Field Museum. The dinosaur is named "Sue" after fossil hunter Susan Hendrickson. Ms. Hendrickson discovered Sue on August 12, 1990, on the Sioux Indian Reservation in South Dakota.

Sue is the most complete *T. rex* skeleton ever found. She is also the best-preserved. The skeleton on display at the Field Museum of Chicago is not a plastic model or a plaster cast. Nor is it made up of skeletons from two or more dinosaurs. Unlike other *T. rex* displays, this one is real.

Sue did not come cheap. Soon after Sue was discovered in 1990, a dispute arose over who really owned her. The owner of the land where Sue was found claimed she belonged to him. Since the land is on the Sioux Indian Reservation, the Sioux believed that she was rightfully theirs. Susan Hendrickson was working with people from the Black Hills Institute when she found Sue. They thought the dinosaur was theirs since "they" had found her. The dispute was finally settled in court five years later. A judge decided that Sue belonged to the landowner, and the landowner decided to put Sue up for sale. The Field Museum paid $8.36 million for Sue in 1997 at an auction in New York City.

Without help from The McDonald's® Corporation and Walt Disney World Resort®, the Field Museum could not have purchased Sue. It was agreed that the Field Museum would get the real bones, and the two companies got rights to make casts of the bones. As a result, a cast of Sue will soon be a permanent display in Dinoland U.S.A. in Disney's Animal Kingdom.

This summer, a lot more people will have a chance to see Sue. McDonald's® is sponsoring two identical Field Museum exhibitions that will travel to cities all over the country. The Field Museum of Chicago is open every day from 9 A.M. to 5 P.M. Admission is $8 for adults and $4 for children ages three to eleven. Wednesdays are free!

For more information about Sue or to find out what cities Sue will be traveling to and when, call the Field Museum or visit their Web site at www.fieldmuseum.org.

1. **The *Tyrannosaurus rex* named Sue was discovered by —**
   - Ⓐ a South Dakota landowner.
   - Ⓑ a fossil hunter.
   - Ⓒ an employee of the Field Museum of Chicago.
   - Ⓓ a Sioux Indian.

2. **When and where was Sue discovered?**

   _____

3. **A judge decided that Sue rightfully belonged to —**
   - Ⓕ the Black Hills Institute.
   - Ⓖ the Sioux Indians.
   - Ⓗ the owner of the land where it was discovered.
   - Ⓙ the Field Museum of Chicago.

4. **How is the *Tyrannosaurus rex* skeleton on display at the Field Museum different from other *T. rex* displays?**

   _____

   _____

5. **Which statement from this article is an opinion?**
   - Ⓐ "Sue is the most complete *T. rex* skeleton ever found."
   - Ⓑ "Sue did not come cheap."
   - Ⓒ "Susan Hendrickson was working with people from the Black Hills Institute."
   - Ⓓ "The Field Museum of Chicago is open every day from 9 A.M. to 5 P.M."

6. **Who helped the Field Museum buy Sue, and what did they get out of the deal?**

   _____

   _____

Text 18 How do you build a tepee?

Building a Tepee

For centuries, tepees have been used as movable shelters. They are fairly easy to build and are quite sturdy, but they are also easy to take down and move to another place. The directions below explain how to build a tepee. Such a skill might come in handy someday if you find yourself in the wilderness without a tent.

You'll need:

12 tepee poles (at least 10 feet long). You can use branches from trees (the branches should be 2 to 3 inches thick at the fat end), or you can buy long wooden poles at a lumberyard. You'll also need about 4 1/2 feet of string or twine, a few feet of rope, and 4 or 5 old sheets, blankets, or tarps.

To build a tepee:

1. Make a tripod by lashing three of the tepee poles together with rope. If you are using tree branches, make sure you lash the branches together about 12 inches from the small ends.

2. Decide where you are going to put your tepee, and then drive a small stick into the ground in the center of where your tepee will be.

3. Tie a piece of string or twine to the stick.

4. From the center stick, measure out four feet of string and tie a sharp stick to the end of the string. The sharp stick will be your "marker" stick.

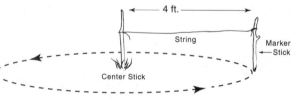

5. Draw the outline for the base of your tepee using the marker stick. Do this by walking in a circle around the center stick while dragging the marker stick on the ground.

6. Take the tripod you made in step 1 and stand it up in the circle. Make sure there is equal distance between each pole around the circle.

7. To make the frame for your tepee, lean the remaining poles against the tripod. Hold the poles in place by setting their top ends inside the "V" above the lashing. Make sure the bottom ends are all equally spaced around the circle.

8. To finish your tepee, cover the frame with old sheets, blankets, or waterproof tarps. Don't forget to leave a space for a door.

Scholastic Professional Books

1. **What is the first step in making a tepee?**
   Ⓐ driving a small stick into the ground
   Ⓑ wrapping the poles with a covering
   Ⓒ drawing a circle on the ground
   Ⓓ making a tripod with three poles

2. **Could you use broom handles as tepee poles? Explain.**

   _____

   _____

3. **What should you do just after you drive a stick into the ground to mark the center of your tepee?**

   _____

   _____

4. **What most likely would happen if the poles for your tepee were not evenly spaced around the circle?**
   Ⓕ The tepee would tilt to one side or tip over.
   Ⓖ The tepee would be too low for anyone to stand up inside.
   Ⓗ There would not be any space for a door.
   Ⓙ You would have to draw another circle.

5. **The directions say you can cover the frame with sheets, blankets, or tarps. Why might tarps be better than sheets or blankets?**

   _____

   _____

Text 19 What was life like for immigrants in the 1930s?

INTERVIEW WITH A GRANITE WORKER

During the late 1930s, writers hired by the federal government recorded the life stories of more than 10,000 men and women throughout the United States, covering a wide range of regions, ethnic groups, and occupations. The plan was one day to publish a series of books that would show everyday life in the United States. Unfortunately, that never happened, but the stories and interviews are stored in the Library of Congress. They are available to anyone interested in reading them. The excerpt below is from an interview with a Vermont granite worker who came to the United States from Italy. The interview was recorded in 1939.

Q. It must have taken courage for a boy of sixteen to leave home—father, mother, brothers, sisters, and cross the ocean to a strange country. Did you have relatives here?

A. Sure it take courage, but what can I do? We live in a small village and there is no work. Only the farm work, and my father and two brothers can take care of that, so I decide to come to America where there is more work and more money. None of my family was over here, only the very good friend of the family, Aldo, who is what you call "promised" to marry my sister. He write that in another year he have enough to send for her. He say he make the money fast by cutting the stone, so after my sister she read the letter to my father and mother, I tease them to let me go, and so here I am. The next year my sister come, so I live with them two, three year. And I see how very happy these two are, just like my father and mother in the old country, so I look around and I see this Lucia who bring the dinner to the shed every day to her brother Paolo. She is dark and her eyes they laugh all the time. One day I make it the business not to go home to the dinner. I take it with me, and when twelve o'clock come, I sit near the brother of Lucia and wait for her to come.

Q. That's how you met your wife. You picked her out and then planned the meeting. You made it easy for yourself.

A. Easy? Who say it is easy to marry Lucia? I wait and pretty soon she come up the hill with a basket on her arm, and she say to the brother, "Paolo, today I make *polenta* for you, if you eat quick it is still hot." I tell them I have not tasted good *polenta* since I leave the old country, but Paolo, he is already busy with the teeth to eat it, and he say nothing and Lucia she is already walking away down the hill. Then I try to be very extra nice to this Paolo so one day he will invite me to the house. I make him a present of a stonecutter's apron, and when I see his red chalk for to mark stone is low, I say, "Here, Paolo, take four, five. I have a big box." But the presents do not take me to his house. Then I listen to the men talk, and they say Paolo is a very jealous brother, and he is afraid to lose his good home if his Lucia marry. . . .

Scholastic Professional Books

Q. You've made me curious. Did you finally meet her? Is Lucia your wife?

A. You wait. You tell me to talk all I want, and say what I want, and talk so long as I want, so you wait. . . . No, that day I do not meet Lucia, nor the next, or the next. And one day I see her stop and talk to a man who is here some four year before me and who is build himself a house and is looking for a wife. I feel very bad and almost I give up, but not quite. Maybe you laugh when I tell you I decide to pray to Santa Lucia who is what you call the name saint of this Lucia. And what do you think happen? One cold day, and slippery, who do you think slip and fall right in front of my sister's house but this Lucia! I run out to help her but already her brother is helping her, so I say quick to my sister, "Go out and tell her to come in, some excuse, any excuse—to dry her clothes, to have the coffee, anything. . ." And so Lucia come in the house. She and my sister, they become good friends, then Lucia and me become good friends, and then more than friends, and then we get married.

Q. It sounds like a book.

A. It is life. If you put life in two covers, what a big book that would be, and so many strange stories you would not believe they are true.

1. **The granite worker came to the United States to —**
   (A) find a wife.
   (B) take care of his sister.
   (C) look for work.
   (D) prove he had courage.

2. **When the granite worker first came to the United States, he lived with —**
   (F) Paolo.
   (G) his mother and father.
   (H) Lucia.
   (J) a friend of the family.

3. **Why was the granite worker extra nice to Paolo?**

   _____

   _____

4. **Describe the events that led to the granite worker's finally meeting Lucia.**

   _____

   _____

   _____

   _____

Text 20 Were there really submarines during the Civil War?

Remembering the *Hunley*

Toward the end of the Civil War, the Union Navy blockaded the port of Charleston, South Carolina. A line of Union warships kept other boats from entering the harbor. Before long, the people of Charleston had to find a way to break the blockade. Enter the *H.L. Hunley*, the world's first successful submarine.

On the night of February 17, 1864, the *Hunley* and its crew of nine men left the coast of South Carolina. The gray iron boat was 39 feet 5 inches long and weighed more than 7 tons. Its hull was 3 feet 10 inches wide and just over 4 feet high. The boat was powered by hand. Eight men sat in a very small space and turned hand cranks to work the boat's propeller. The captain, Lieutenant George Dixon, looked through a glass window in the top hatch to steer the boat. He used dive planes on the sides of the boat to control how deep it went. On the front of the *Hunley* was a torpedo. It was attached to an iron rod with a barb on the end.

Unlike today's submarines, the *Hunley* did not have a motor, electricity, or light. When the boat was underwater, there was no way to bring in fresh air. The crew of the *Hunley* lit a candle when the boat submerged, and the candle provided the only light. The candle flame also burned oxygen. When the candle flickered and went out, the men knew it was time to get back to the surface before they ran out of air.

On that night in 1864, the *Hunley's* mission was to sink the Union's largest ship, the U.S.S. *Housatonic*. Under cover of darkness, the *Hunley* traveled four miles from the coast and rammed straight into the side of the *Housatonic*. The barbed iron rod stuck into the warship's hull. Then the crew of the *Hunley* reversed the propeller and paddled backward away from the *Housatonic*. A 150-foot rope attached to the torpedo played out as the *Hunley* backed off. When the *Hunley* reached the end of the rope, the torpedo exploded. It blew a huge hole in the *Housatonic's* side. Within minutes, the *Housatonic* sank to the bottom, and its crew of 155 men was thrown into the water.

As the *Hunley* moved away, the hatch on the top of the boat opened, and Lieutenant Dixon shined a blue light. This was a signal to men waiting on shore that the mission had been successful. For the first time in history, a submarine had sunk an enemy ship.

With its job done, the *Hunley* headed for shore—but it never arrived. For reasons unknown, the *Hunley* sank that night off the coast of South Carolina. It was not seen again for 131 years.

In 1995, a group of searchers found the *Hunley* on the ocean floor near the coast. It lay under 30 feet of water and several feet of silt. It was very well preserved, and it still contained the remains of its brave crew.

After many years of effort and careful planning, the *Hunley* was raised from the sea on August 8, 2000, and taken to Charleston. There, the long-lost boat will be restored in a seven-year process and then will be displayed in the Charleston Museum. The remains of the crew will be buried in Charleston's Magnolia Cemetery with military honors. And the *H.L. Hunley* will take its rightful place in naval history.

1.   **What did the *Hunley* do on February 17, 1864? Write a brief summary.**

_____

_____

_____

_____

2.   **When the blue light signal was given by the *Hunley*, it meant that —**
   Ⓐ the *Housatonic* had been sunk.
   Ⓑ all the crew's oxygen was gone.
   Ⓒ the torpedo was ready to explode.
   Ⓓ all crew members were safe.

3.   **How was the *Hunley* different from today's submarines? Name two or three ways it was different.**

_____

_____

_____

_____

Text 21 How do you make a crossword puzzle?

Across and Down

Did you know that an *oryx* is an African antelope with straight horns? Did you know that an *arete* is a mountain ridge formed by glaciers? That a *naira* is a unit of money in Nigeria? If you happen to be a person who likes crossword puzzles, you will probably run into these words and many more that are just as unusual. If not, then you may never see these words again. They are not exactly the kinds of words you would use in everyday conversation, but I have always had a certain fondness for them.

I knew from an early age that I wanted to be a writer, and I loved to solve crossword puzzles. Perhaps it was <u>inevitable</u> that I would begin writing my own puzzles. My original plan was to write novels and win the Nobel Prize for literature, but the first things I ever got published were crossword puzzles. I would sit for hours and hours at the kitchen table trying to think of words that would fit into the puzzles I made. Quite often I would visit the dictionary for help, and I would find words I had never heard of before.

Constructing crossword puzzles is not as difficult as it seems, but it does take a lot of time. First, you have to think of an idea, or theme, for the puzzle. For example, you might decide that the puzzle will focus on the names of states. You choose the states you want to include, and then you build a diagram, like the ones used for puzzles in the newspaper. Crossword puzzles come in certain sizes, and the diagrams are always symmetrical. That means that there are certain patterns of black squares and white squares. If the first word across the top is six letters long, then the last word along the bottom must also be six letters long.

Once you have the diagram and the theme words, then you fill in the rest of the words in the puzzle. Since all the words must fit together across and down, you really need to know some unusual words. For example, let's say you need a five-letter word, and you know the middle letters have to be *a-i-a*. The word could be *naiad*, which is the name for a water nymph from Greek mythology. How often do you think you would see that word? When the words have all been filled in, then you number the squares in the diagram and write a clue for each word.

After several years of writing crossword puzzles for the *Boston Globe, The New York Times*, and many other newspapers and magazines, I finally did start writing novels and stories. But crosswords got me started, and they taught me a vast number of words that I may never see again. As for the Nobel Prize? Well, I did use the word *Nobel* several times in crossword puzzles. . . .

Scholastic Professional Books

1. **What kind of selection is this?**
    Ⓐ realistic fiction
    Ⓑ autobiography
    Ⓒ folktale
    Ⓓ textbook article

2. **The selection says, "Perhaps it was <u>inevitable</u> that I would begin writing my own puzzles." What does <u>inevitable</u> mean?**
    Ⓕ equal on both sides
    Ⓖ interesting in an odd way
    Ⓗ filled with joy
    Ⓙ unable to be avoided

3. **Name two places where you are likely to find the words *oryx* and *naira*.**

_____

_____

4. **What are the major steps in constructing a crossword puzzle?**

_____

_____

_____

_____

5. **What do you think the author of this selection enjoyed most about making crossword puzzles?**

_____

_____

Rolling Stones

WALES—Nearly every day for the past six months, a ragtag group of volunteers has been pushing and pulling a large blue stone through dirt and mud. The stone weighs three tons, and it comes from the Preseli Mountains in southwestern Wales. The group's goal is to move the stone 240 miles across land and water to the Salisbury plain in England. There, the stone will be <u>reunited</u> with its long-lost cousins at a place called Stonehenge.

About 5,000 years ago, people in what is now Britain began building a mysterious circle of blue stones. The building of Stonehenge probably took hundreds of years to complete. The structure has 80 stones in all. Each stone weighs about three tons, and archaeologists believe that all of the stones were transported from Wales to Salisbury.

The goal of this year's stone-moving project is to prove that it would have been possible for the people of long ago to move the stones to Salisbury. The group has used wooden sleds, logs, barges, and pure physical strength to move one stone many miles. Group leader Philip Bowen believes the effort will take a total of almost nine months.

Stonehenge has attracted and mystified people for centuries. No one is sure why it was built, but its design was apparently based on the movement of the sun. Its 80 stones are arranged in a circular design with one stone—the "heel stone"—set apart. Many of the stones stand upright with horizontal stones laid across the top to form arches. If you stand in the center of the circle on the summer or winter solstice (the longest and shortest days of the year), the sun sets directly over the heel stone. For the rest of the year, the sunset moves to different parts of the circle.

Scientists have invented many theories to explain Stonehenge. Some people think it was a calendar used to keep track of days and years. Some think it was a monument for sun worship, or perhaps a monument where people went to honor the dead. Others think that aliens who visited Earth thousands of years ago left Stonehenge behind just to let us know they were here.

For whatever reason it was built, Stonehenge continues to amaze people who see it. Every year on the solstice, thousands of people go to Stonehenge to dance and celebrate. Now Philip Bowen and his group of volunteers are rolling a new stone across the country. They will deliver the stone to Stonehenge, and then . . . well, then they will stop.

Scholastic Professional Books

1. **Which would be another good title for this article?**
   Ⓐ "Sun Worship"
   Ⓑ "Riding a Wooden Sled"
   Ⓒ "Visiting Wales"
   Ⓓ "Moving Stones to Stonehenge"

2. **Why is the group of volunteers moving a three-ton stone?**
   Ⓕ The circle at Stonehenge is missing one stone.
   Ⓖ They want to prove it can be done.
   Ⓗ This last stone will explain the purpose of Stonehenge.
   Ⓙ They want the stone to have a proper home.

3. **The article says, "The stone will be <u>reunited</u> with its long-lost cousins at a place called Stonehenge." Why does the author say the stones will be <u>reunited</u>?**

   _____

   _____

4. **Some information about Stonehenge is fact, and some is theory. In the chart below, write notes in the correct boxes.**

Information About Stonehenge	
Fact	Theory
1.	1.
2.	2.
3.	3.

Text 23 Can herbs really help you feel better?

Herbal Remedies

Did you know that many common plants can be used as medicine? People have been using herbal remedies for centuries—since long before anyone invented aspirin or Band-Aids. You have to be careful, though. Some herbs can be beneficial when used correctly, but harmful when administered improperly. The chart below lists some common herbs used as remedies—and some cautions about their uses.

Herbs	Uses	Cautions
aloe	The leaves of the aloe plant contain a clear gel that helps soothe burns, insect bites, frostbite, wounds, and sunburn.	Aloe should only be applied externally.
eucalyptus	Eucalyptus is a common ingredient in cough drops, nasal sprays, and decongestants. Tea made from eucalyptus leaves can help ease fever, cough, and other cold symptoms. The dried leaves can also be used in room fresheners.	Never ingest eucalyptus oil—it can be poisonous.
meadowsweet	The buds of the meadowsweet plant contain salicin, the same ingredient used in aspirin. Meadowsweet helps ease the pain of headaches and flu. It also smells good and can be used as a room freshener.	
peppermint	Peppermint is used as a flavoring in many things, from chewing gum to toothpaste. Tea made from peppermint soothes the stomach and aids digestion, relieves coughs and congestion, and freshens breath.	Peppermint can sometimes cause harmful reactions in children. Do not give it to children under five.
witch hazel	Witch hazel water made from the leaves or twigs of the witch hazel tree is a good remedy for healing cuts, bruises, and sore muscles.	Witch hazel should only be used externally. If skin irritation results, discontinue use.

1. **The main purpose of this selection is to —**
   Ⓐ explain the history of medicine.
   Ⓑ persuade people to try herbal remedies.
   Ⓒ give information about plants used as medicine.
   Ⓓ tell an entertaining story about plants.

2. **Why does the chart include a column labeled "Cautions"?**

   _____

   _____

3. **How are eucalyptus and meadowsweet alike? Name two similarities.**

   _____

   _____

4. **Which herbs listed in the chart should only be used on the skin?**

   _____

5. **Suppose you just ate a huge dinner, and your stomach is upset. Which herb on the chart would be most helpful to you? Explain.**

   _____

   _____

River Man

hen Chad Pregracke was a teenager in East Moline, Illinois, he and his father lived and worked on the Mississippi River—or rather, in it. Every day they dove into the river to collect freshwater mussels, which they sold to Japanese customers. The river was their <u>livelihood</u>, but Chad came to realize that it was also filthy. While searching for mussels on the river bottom, Chad could not see much because the water was too muddy. But he felt hundreds of objects in the mud that were not mussels: old shoes, toaster ovens, car tires, rusted gas tanks, and all sorts of other junk. When Chad Pregracke was in college, he decided that he had to clean up the river. And that's what he has done.

In the summer of 1997, Chad started the Mississippi River Beautification & Restoration Project. Using a 20-foot motorboat and working mainly by himself, Chad cleaned up 100 miles of shoreline in Illinois and Iowa. By summer's end, he had removed and recycled 45,000 pounds of trash! As people learned about Chad's efforts, they began to offer help. Towns and companies along the river donated money and equipment, and communities pitched in by holding cleanup days.

In 1998, the project grew. Chad fixed up two barges and a sort of tugboat, and he hired a crew. During the summer months, Chad and his crew cleaned up 900 miles of Mississippi shoreline from St. Louis, Missouri, to Guttenberg, Iowa. They collected 400,000 pounds of trash—everything from old refrigerators to lawn mowers to plastic legs!

In the next year, Chad's group completed the cleanup of more than 1,000 miles of the Mississippi River. They also established an "Adopt a Mississippi River Mile" program. In this program, companies and groups took responsibility for keeping parts of the river clean. After that, Chad started on the Illinois River.

Today, Chad Pregracke's project has many corporate sponsors and an annual budget of $200,000. Chad also has ambitious plans. When he has done what he can for the Mississippi and Illinois rivers, he will move eastward. He wants to clean up the Ohio River next, and then perhaps the Hudson. You can go to his Web site at <u>www.cleanrivers.com</u> to check on his progress and see what he is doing. Chad's heroic efforts are paying off, and maybe he will inspire others to join his project or go out and start their own. There is no shortage of rivers and other places that need cleaning up.

1. **If this article appeared in a newspaper, which would be the best headline for the article?**
   Ⓐ "Old Refrigerators Turn to Trash"
   Ⓑ "There Is Money in That River!"
   Ⓒ "Chad Pregracke Cleans Up River"
   Ⓓ "Spend Summers With Chad Pregracke"

2. **How does the map help you understand this article?**

   _____

   _____

3. **The article says, "The river was their <u>livelihood</u>." What does the word <u>livelihood</u> mean?**

   _____

   _____

4. **Why does the author mention <u>www.cleanrivers.com</u> in this article?**

   _____

   _____

5. **Do you think that Chad Pregracke is a hero? Write a brief paragraph telling why you think he is or is not a hero.**

   _____

   _____

   _____

   _____

   _____

Answer Key

1. Eating Bugs
1. B
2. Answers will vary. Students might describe Aletheia Price as unusual, interesting, curious, admirable, adventurous, or something similar because she eats insects and seems to enjoy them.

2. Letter to the Editor
1. B
2. F
3. Examples: The skate park will help prevent accidents on the sidewalks and streets; kids will enjoy having a park; kids will have a place to go; it will not cost much to build; skateboarding is good exercise.

3. Bearded Dragons
1. C
2. F
3. Answers will vary. Students should tell whether they think a bearded dragon would be a good pet for them or not, and should give at least one reason.

4. Captain Cammi
1. A
2. J
3. Examples: She was the captain of Team USA; she was on the team that won the Gold Medal in 1998; she was the all-time leading scorer at Providence; she led her team to two national championships; she was chosen ECAC Player of the Year for three straight years; she became a radio commentator.
4. Examples: Watching her brother Tony gave her the dream of playing in the Olympics; playing with her brothers made her a great hockey player.

5. Feng Shui
1. B
2. H
3. Example: Success in life derives from the location or arrangement of your home and/or place of business.
4. B

5. Answers will vary. Students should give their opinions with supporting details.

6. Making Gazpacho
1. Answers will vary. Gazpacho is certainly "colorful"; it contains red tomatoes and pimientos and green peppers. It is also "spicy," since it contains Tabasco sauce, onions, garlic, and chives.
2. You should save the garlic so it can be crushed and added to the soup (in step 5).

7. The Leaning Tower
1. D
2. F
3. The answer should indicate that the tower is sinking faster on one side than on the other, or it is settling into the ground unevenly.

8. *Chicken Run*
1. B
2. H
3. Answers will vary. Students should state yes or no and give a reason.

9. Speech to the One Hundred Sixty-Sixth Ohio Regiment
1. to thank the soldiers for their efforts
2. Any of their children could become president of the United States, as he had.
3. to maintain our free government, or to ensure that everyone has a fair and equal chance in life

10. Vermont Foliage Video
1. B
2. F
3. Example: Send your name and address to the address given with a check for $19.95 plus $5.00 shipping and handling.
4. Examples: Autumn foliage, Mount Mansfield, Camel's Hump, Lake Champlain, Green Mountain State Forest, the lakes of the Northeast Kingdom, Bennington battle site, Coolidge's birthplace.
5. The company will refund the purchase price.

11. Tulipomania
1. C
2. G
3. Example: After Clusius brought some bulbs to Holland, some "businessmen" stole his bulbs and began raising tulips. When rich people saw the beautiful flowers, demand for the bulbs increased, and so did the prices. Prices continued to rise until 1637 when a group of tulip merchants suddenly could not sell their bulbs. Word spread, and the tulip craze ended.

12. Learning From History
1. B
2. J
3. C
4. Answers may vary. Examples: The people learned that they should pay attention to weather warnings, that they should not build houses and other structures on the shore, or that they should have more respect for the power of nature.
5. Answers will vary. The author seems to think that these people are foolish because they are taking an unnecessary risk and are ignoring the dangers of hurricanes.

13. Letter From Harry Truman
1. C
2. F
3. nothing
4. He didn't think people should steal Bibles; it would be "sacrilegious"; or, it would be worse than stealing just about anything else.
5. Example: It was snowing out, and two inches of snow had already fallen. It had been a hard winter.
6. He hoped she would write a letter back to him.

14. The King of Soccer
1. D
2. He is the only person to have played on three winning World Cup teams.
3. G
4. It is the name of the street he lived on as a child; it is the name of his neighborhood soccer team; it is Brazil's Independence Day; it was the day he played his first professional soccer game with the Santos.

15. Fireworks
1. D
2. F
3. D
4. They cause pollution; they contain harmful chemicals; they can damage your hearing; they can lead to injuries and even death.
5. The author believes all consumer fireworks should be banned, but it's okay for people to continue enjoying public fireworks displays.
6. G

16. Funny Money
1. C
2. Examples: Colonial bills were easy to copy; each colony issued its own bills; banks printed many different kinds of bills, so fake ones were hard to spot.
3. G
4. D
5. Examples: Special ink that changes color; security threads; microprinted words; larger portraits that are off center; watermarks that can be seen from both sides when held up to a light.

17. Traveling Sue
1. B
2. on August 12, 1990, on the Sioux Indian Reservation in South Dakota
3. H
4. It is larger and more complete than any other T. rex skeleton; the real skeleton is on display.
5. B
6. The McDonald's® Corporation and Walt Disney World Resort® helped buy Sue. In return, they got rights to make casts of its bones.

18. Building a Tepee
1. D
2. No, they are not long enough. You could not stand up in the tepee.
3. Tie a piece of string or twine to the stick.
4. F
5. Tarps are waterproof, but sheets or blankets are not.

19. Interview With a Granite Worker
1. C
2. J
3. He hoped to get invited to Paolo's house so he could meet Lucia.
4. Answers may vary. Lucia slipped and fell on some ice in front of the granite worker's sister's house. He ran out to help, but her brother was already helping her. The granite worker urged his sister to run out and invite her inside. Lucia came into the house.

20. Remembering the *Hunley*
1. Example: The *Hunley* rammed the Union ship *Housatonic*, exploded a torpedo, and sank the ship. Then the *Hunley* disappeared.
2. A
3. Examples: The *Hunley* did not have power, electricity, or light; it was powered by hand; it had no way to bring in fresh air, so it could only stay underwater as long as the air lasted.

21. Across and Down
1. B
2. J
3. in crossword puzzles and in dictionaries
4. Responses should include at least four steps. Example: (1) Think of an idea, or theme; (2) choose words to fit the theme; (3) make a diagram; (4) fill in words; (5) number the boxes; (6) write the clues.
5. learning new words, or the challenge of finding words that fit

22. Rolling Stones
1. D
2. G
3. Archaeologists believe that the stones at Stonehenge all came from the same place in Wales, and the "new" stone comes from there, too.
4. Examples of Fact: Stonehenge has 80 stones. The stones are arranged in a circle. The stones came from Wales. Its design is based on the movement of the sun. It is located in Salisbury, England.
   Examples of Theory: Stonehenge was a calendar. It was a monument for sun worship. It was a monument to honor the dead. Aliens built it. Possibly, the stones came from Wales.

23. Herbal Remedies
1. C
2. Some of these herbs can be harmful if used incorrectly.
3. Both help to ease cold or flu symptoms; both can be used as room fresheners.
4. aloe and witch hazel
5. Peppermint would be most useful because it soothes the stomach and aids digestion.

24. River Man
1. C
2. Example: It helps you visualize the areas where Chad Pregracke worked, or it helps you appreciate the size of the job he has done.
3. source of income or way to make a living
4. It is a Web site about Chad Pregracke's project; you can go there for more information about Pregracke.
5. Answers will vary. Students should support their opinions.